MICHELLE KWAN

My Special Moments

VOLO

HYPERION
NEW YORK

Copyright © 2001 by Michelle Kwan Corp.
Volo and the Volo colophon are trademarks of Disney Enterprises, Inc.

Photo credits are found on the last page of the book.
Printed in the United States of America
First Edition
1 3 5 7 9 10 8 6 4 2

Interior designed by Paul Colin/Cezanne Studio
This book is set in Tekton.
ISBN 0-7868-1580-9
Visit www.volobooks.com
The UCLA logo is shown courtesy of University of California, Los Angeles.
The Children's Miracle Network logo is shown courtesy of The Children's Miracle Network.

Hi, I'm Michelle Kwan. This is my photo album, filled with my favorite memories. I've had an amazing time over the last few years. My life has been like a whirlwind!

I love my life, and I'm excited to share it with you.

I am a very competitive person. My personal motto is Work hard, be yourself, and have fun. And for me, the competition is the fun part. That's why I decided to keep my Olympic-eligible status after the 1998 Nagano Olympics. I'm not sticking around just to have another chance at Olympic gold. It's not about the medal—it's about the skating. I still have so much I want to accomplish as a skater. The challenge of competition really pushes me to try new things and give it my all.

My coach, Frank Carroll, and I have a few rituals before I compete. We try to go someplace away from everyone, and he shares his last words of advice with me. I do stretches to keep my muscles from cooling down after the warm-up, and I close my eyes and picture myself skating a perfect program.

When I am on the ice, I have to focus. I want to lose myself in the music, but I have to keep enough control to land all of my jumps and get through other tricky moves.

Designing a Program

The skating season starts in the fall, and I usually compete in at least one event every month between October and March. Nationals are in January or February, and Worlds are in March. And once every four years, the Olympics fall between Nationals and Worlds.

As soon as one competitive season ends, it's time to start thinking about my programs for the next season. I need three new programs every year: my short, technical program; the long program, which is also called the free skate; and another program for exhibitions and tours.

Luckily, I don't have to create these all by myself. Frank and I work with choreographers to create programs that express my style and skill.

Frank and me talking before a program

My choreographer, Frank, and I listen to hundreds of CDs to find just the right kind of music. We try to find something a little unusual that no other skaters have used. I want my programs to be as original as they can be.

Music is the most important element in skating—it inspires every jump, every stroke of the blade, every tilt of the head. It tells me what to do and how to feel.

I really have to love our musical selections because between competitions and daily practices I'll listen to them thousands of times during the year.

Once we decide on music, I work with the choreographer to imagine what moves work best with the fast and slow parts. We discuss where to put the jumps and think about footwork and spins and spirals. It's a long process. Sometimes we'll spend one hour deciding what I'll do for about two seconds of the program!

It's Frank's job to watch over this process. He'll give us his opinion. Sometimes he'll even suggest a new move he thinks I should add to a program. It was Frank's idea to put the Charlotte spiral in my "Ariane" long program. Now it's one of my favorite moves.

After a lot of thought, we always come up with wonderful ways of expressing how the music makes us feel. It usually takes about two weeks to get the new programs in good shape.

The Charlotte spiral is one of my favorite moves.

7

Highlights on Ice

1999–2001 Highlights

A Day in the Life (short program)
  Music: "A Day in the Life," written by John Lennon and
  Paul McCartney and performed by Jeff Beck

When I skated this program:

1999 Masters of Figure Skating
1999 Skate America
1999 Skate Canada
2000 Japan Open
2000 Grand Prix Finals
2000 US Nationals
2000 World Championships

Since I was named after the song "Michelle" by the Beatles, it seems logical that I would like the band. I especially liked skating to the Beatles' "A Day in the Life," because there is so much going on in it. There are a lot of different emotions and effects in the music.

Le Violin Rouge (long program)

Music: Selections from "The Red Violin" soundtrack
composed by John Corigliano with Joshua Bell, violin

When I skated this program:

1999 Skate America
1999 Skate Canada
2000 Grand Prix Finals
2000 US Nationals
2000 World Championships

There's something very compelling about this music. The mystery of it really holds the program together. When I performed at Worlds, it was the first time I went out on the ice and pushed and pushed through the entire four minutes. I wouldn't let myself hold anything back. I never felt so fast.

East of Eden (Exhibition and short program)
Music: Finale from the "East of Eden" miniseries, composed by Lee Holdridge

When I skated this program:

1996 US Nationals
1996 World Championships
1998 Grand Slam
1998 Masters of Figure Skating
1998 World Pro
1999 Japan Open
1999 US Nationals
1999 World Championships
2000 Canadian Open
2001 US Nationals
2001 Grand Prix Finals
2001 World Championships

I've skated to this music during several different seasons. I think it is wonderful. I first used it as an exhibition piece. Then, I decided to mold it into a short program during the 2000/2001 season. I was looking for something I could really relate to—something that matched my mood and skating at the time. It was very comforting to return to the music in 2000, like a favorite memory.

Beautiful World (exhibition and interpretive long program)
Music: "Beautiful World," composed
by Julie Gold and performed by Sumi Jo

When I skated this program:

2000 Figure Skating Classic
2000 Masters of Figure Skating
2000 Skate America
2000 Skate Canada
2000 Canadian Open
2000 Figure Skating Challenge
2001 Grand Prix Final
2001 World Championships

I found the lyrics
to this music so
inspiring—it's
about changing
the world for the
better in one day
if you only had
the chance.

Song of the Black Swan (long program)

Music: "Song of the Black Swan," composed by Heitor Villa-Lobos
with Julian Lloyd Webber, cello
"Dumky," from *Lento maestoso*
Piano Trio in E, op. 90 by Antonin Dvorák

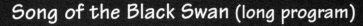

When I skated this program:

2000 Skate America
2000 Skate Canada
2001 US Nationals
2001 Grand Prix Finals
2001 World Championships

Each season, I want to set new challenges for myself. With seven triples, including a triple toe/triple toe combination, this program really challenged me to focus and maintain my speed.

My favorite part comes at the end, when I do a split jump that leads right into a spread eagle that just folds into a death drop spin.

Winning my fourth World Championship was a dream come true. *

Training

To stay at the top of my sport, I have to keep a very strict training schedule. On top of that, I have other things I want to do, too. Every day is jam-packed.

In order to be at my best when I compete, I push myself every time I hit the ice. I have a rigorous training schedule to keep in shape and sharpen my technique. I always want to be increasing my skill—just like a runner always wants to clock a faster sprint time.

Every day I have three one-hour skating sessions. At the beginning of each session, I decide what I want to work on: a special jump, my spins, or some new footwork for a program. I set a goal that I will practice that move until I have it down, until it's perfect. When I'm in a competition, I want to feel like my program is the most natural thing in the world for me. It takes a lot of work to make it look that easy.

I also do off-ice training. Stretching is always important because it keeps your muscles loose while strengthening them as well. You might not think of figure skating as a sport that requires a lot of strength, but it does—every jump and spin takes your upper-body, leg, and stomach muscles to complete the rotations and maintain speed. Weight training and running help, too.

My skates can really affect how I skate. My dad will work on the skates, building up and shaving down the heels, and adjusting the blades. It can take months to totally break in a new pair of skates.

Off the Ice

Even though skating takes up a lot of my time, I make time for other things—like school. You might think school is not your idea of free time, but getting a good education has always been one of my top goals. I enrolled at UCLA in the fall of 1999.

My sister Karen and me during Winter Break

I find it hard balancing both school and skating, but I don't think either one can wait. It's not easy being a student and an athlete, but I've developed a schedule that lets me concentrate on the books and the ice, equally. But it's nice to take a break with friends and family. Even though my schedule is so busy, I do find time to go out with friends and spend time with my boyfriend.

When I'm not on the ice I like to Rollerblade, watch movies, shop, cook, chat online with friends, and read.

"She shoots. She scores!"

Fave movies to rent:

GLADIATOR

TITANIC

THE CUTTING EDGE

JERRY MAGUIRE

BRAVEHEART

Fave Foods:

Junior Mints

Sushi

Chocolate

Frozen Yogurt

My Family

My family is very important to me. They have believed in me from the first time I pulled on a skate. But more important, they give me a sense of balance. They let me know that skating isn't everything, and that we'll all support each other, no matter what.

Here I am as a baby. I was born July 7th 1980.

Karen takes top prize!

Karen and I have shared just about everything—especially our love for skating. When we first started skating we were so excited for our morning lessons that we would sometimes sleep in our skating outfits.

Who looks more serious?

I'm very lucky being the youngest in my family. I've always had someone to look out for me—thanks to my sister, Karen, and my brother, Ron.

Being on the ice comes naturally to all of us.

Mom and I are flying high!

My mom gives me faith in myself and my dreams. She has so much confidence in me. When I need extra strength, I know I can turn to her. We understand each other extremely well because we're a lot alike.

My dad is a very smart man. He has a great way of looking at the world. He also gives great advice. When I went through a

tough year on the ice in 1997, he's the one who helped me figure out what I had to do. He helped me realize that my love for skating was stronger than my love for winning.

We love having big dinners together when we are all home.

My brother and me playing street hockey

Hanging out with my family in Lake Arrowhead

In this shot, you can see the necklace my grandmother gave me. It has a Chinese dragon on it—a symbol for luck. I started wearing it when I was ten years old and I never take it off.

21

Off-Season

After the competitions are over, I skate in the John Hancock Champions on Ice Tour and other exhibitions. The tours are a great way to wind down after the stress of competing. You get to practice every day and skate in front of thousands of people every night. And there are no judges!

Since no judges are there, we all try new things in our exhibition programs. Plus, it allows you to express yourself when you skate to music with words.

I skated to music from the James Bond film "The World Is Not Enough" in Champions on Ice 2000.

The other great part about the tour is getting to wear creative costumes that we normally don't wear during competitions.

Aren't these feathers wild?

Skating in Champions on Ice 2001

My Shows

One of my favorite memories is when I worked on my very own skating specials. My first Disney special was "Reflections on Ice: Michelle Kwan Skates to the Music of Mulan." When I was young, my parents told me the story of Mulan. She was an independent, dedicated, and strong-minded teenager. I really respect and relate to her.

Here I am in battle gear with Philippe Candeloro and Michael Weiss.

My second special was "Disney's Greatest Hits." It's fun to skate to the songs from movies I remember when I was younger.

The best part of this television special was taking to the ice with so many talented skaters. Here I am with Ilia Kulik and Elvis Stojko. They are both magnificent skaters, natural performers, and great friends.

It was fun to pick out music for the show.

Here I am as Ariel. I have to admit that I would never want to be a mermaid. I love to swim, but I really don't like the ocean. Besides, without legs, how would I skate?

In my third Disney special, "Michelle Kwan: Princess on Ice," I skated with legends Dorothy Hamill and Katarina Witt for the first time. It was an amazing experience! We had a great time and got to wear really fun outfits.

I'm a Princess! Look at that hairstyle!

Dancing with O TOWN in my TV special!

Photo Shoots

I still can't believe I was named one of *People* magazine's 50 Most Beautiful People.

The photo shoot was so cool. I'm really on an ice chair!

In January 2001, I was on the cover of *Sports Illustrated for Women.* Whenever I do a photo shoot, there are always people fixing my hair and doing my makeup. I love it!

Photo shoots are hard work, but I still try to have fun.

I can't believe how many people it took to make a TV commercial.

Taking a break between shoots

What a hair-raising experience!

Here I am in New York for the Goodwill Games.
I love New York!

My Fans

My fans are so important to me. Their enthusiasm and support help me with my skating. It really is nice to have such fantastic fans.

I get so many stuffed animals from my fans after I skate a program. I appreciate the gifts and love them all. But I can't keep all of them either. After each competition I donate the stuffed animals to a local children's hospital.

Reaching Out

Children's
Miracle ⬥ Network®
hospitals helping kids

The Children's Miracle Network raises funds and awareness for children's hospitals all over North America. I feel really proud to be the spokesperson for their "Champions Across America" program.

Teachers are very special! I was honored to be a presenter at Disney's American Teacher Awards with my sister, Karen.

In the Spotlight

I was a guest star on *Sabrina the Teenage Witch*. Melissa Joan Hart was super cool and so nice.

I couldn't believe it when I heard that there would be a wax statue of me at Madame Tussaud's New York Wax Museum, but you can see all 5'2" of me.

Which one is the real me?

I was invited to the White House for an official state dinner. Wow! I met President Clinton and Hillary Rodham Clinton. It was such an honor, and the food was incredible, too!

Outtakes

I spend most of my time on the ice, but I'm in front of the cameras a lot.

I try to have a good time at photo shoots and skating specials. Here I am behind the scenes.

Here I am filming a TV commercial!

I study videos of my new programs backstage.

This was a fun number!

Goofing around in practice
with SheDaisy's Kassidy
during my TV special

1997 Nationals

1998 Worlds

1997 Champions on Ice

1996 Worlds

1998 Olympics

1998 World Pro

1999 Figure Skating Classic

39

1999 Skate America

2000 Skate America

2000 Nationals

2001 Nationals

2000 Skate America

2001 Worlds

41

Looking Ahead

I've learned that focusing on what I need to do works much better than thinking about what I shouldn't do. It keeps me positive.

When I was younger I never realized there would be so many challenges, but now I know that learning to deal with them is often the key to success.

More than any of the medals I've won, what I cherish most of all is my skating itself.

People sometimes ask me what I want my lasting impact on figure skating to be. I want to be more than someone who did a lot of triples. When people think of me, I'd like them to remember an emotion— the way they felt when they watched me skate. If I can give them a memory of that happiness, that is more than I could ever hope for. And if I can always have the happiness that skating brings me, it would be a dream come true.